Heir Today— Gone Tomorrow

A Comedy

Chris Petz

Samuel French—London
New York — Sydney — Toronto — Hollywood

CHARACTERS

Billy, a young man
Pat, a young woman
Shoesmith, a solicitor
P.C. Carter, a young policeman
Nigel Branson, a telegram boy
Jane Robinson, a solicitor's secretary
Margarette Nelson, Billy's mother
Annie, a young woman

The action takes place in the sitting-room and kitchen of a bachelor flat

ACT I   Morning
ACT II   Immediately following
ACT III Some time later

Time—the present

ACT I

The sitting-room/kitchen of a bachelor flat. Morning

*There is a small alcove upstage which houses a sink and small cooker, etc—
the kitchen area. This alcove has a curtain which can be drawn across. There
are two doors to the sitting-room: one leads off to a bedroom, the other
is the front door. There is also a sliding door which, when opened, reveals
a cupboard for coats, etc. The general appearance of the room shows that
a party has taken place the night before. Bottles and other remnants are
scattered around. There is a settee with blankets covering it.*

After the CURTAIN *rises the phone begins to ring. As it does so, the pile
of blankets on the sofa begins to move. Eventually a young girl, Pat, sticks
her head out. She emerges from beneath the blankets, revealing that she is
dressed only in pants and a bra. She stands, clutches her head, and sits again.
It is obvious that she has a hangover. She shakes her head and gingerly stands
again. She staggers round, looking under cushions, etc.*

Pat All right, all right, I'm trying to find you. (*She continues searching*)
Where is the bloody phone?

The phone stops ringing. Pat shrugs and sits on the sofa

Oh boy. What a party! (*She stands*) Oh! What a hangover!! (*She searches
amongst the glasses*) Not a clean glass in the place. Still, hardly surprising.
(*She picks up a half-full glass and pours the contents into another glass,
which she puts down*) Now, where does he keep the Andrews? (*She looks
around, spots the kitchen area, goes there and searches on a shelf, looking
in various bottles and tins of different sizes*) Let's see. Instant mash,
baked beans, baked beans, creamed rice, baked beans, baked beans. If
he lives on that he MUST have some Andrews. baked beans, baked
beans-ah! Andrews. Success.

She closes the curtain, and the phone begins to ring again

Go on, ring. I don't care. I don't live here anyway!

The phone continues to ring

Billy (*off*) All right, all right, I'm coming.

*Billy appears in the bedroom door. He is equally hung over and has a sheet
wrapped around him. Around his neck he wears a chain on which is hung
a key*

(*Searching*) Where's the damned phone gone?

The phone stops ringing as he finds it

All right, see if I care. (*He sits on the sofa and groans, clutching his head. After a moment he looks up, enlightened*) Andrews! That's what I need. A good strong dose of liver salts to liven up the system, to clear the head, to add a sparkle to the day, to make things go with a bang! (*He stands suddenly*) Oh! (*He clutches his head. He looks for an empty glass but there is not one. He finds one half full, looks at it, sniffs it, pulls a face and empties the glass into the one Pat poured some into earlier. He goes to the kitchen area, walks behind the curtain and sees Pat*) Oh sorry! I beg your pardon. (*He walks away, and stops*) There's a half-naked woman in my kitchen!

Pat (*drawing back the curtain*) Good morning. I'm Pat.

Billy Er—good morning. Um—I'm Billy. Er—what are you doing . . .

Pat Helping myself to your Andrews. I'm afraid there's not much left now. Would you like me to mix some up for you? (*Taking his glass and going to the kitchen*) Or, on the other hand I could open a tin of beans, there seem to be plenty here.

Billy (*with a sickly look*) No thank you. The Andrews will be fine.

Pat (*mixing drink and bringing it out*) Or there again, what about a good stiff Scotch? They do say that a hair of the dog that bit you works wonders.

Billy (*taking the drink*) The way I feel at the moment, the dog that bit me deserves a kick in the teeth.

Pat (*laughing*) Yes, I should think you're right. That was some party we had last night. What were we celebrating?

Billy My birthday, I suppose. I'm twenty-one today. But I didn't arrange a party. (*Looking round*) How did all this happen? I don't remember too much . . .

Pat I'm not surprised. Do you remember coming into the pub?

Billy Yes. Yes, I remember that. I'd just had my tea.

Pat Beans, mashed potato and rice?

Billy Yes. How did you know?

Pat Oh—feminine intuition. Anyway, carry on. You'd finished sampling Egon Ronay's suggested meal for one and decided to pop down to the *Pear Tree* for a couple of pints.

Billy Yes. There was quite a crowd there. A couple of people I knew by sight, but I still don't see how that led to me holding a party.

Pat Well, when we arrived at the pub it looked as though you were in a pretty festive mood.

Billy We?

Pat Me and the girls. Carol, one of the girls from work, is getting married so we went out on a hen party.

Billy And when you arrived at the *Pear Tree* I was already quite merry?

Pat Without putting too fine a point on it, you were almost paralytic. There was a gang of blokes on a stag night and you were in the centre of them with a pint pot on your head doing the fan dance with two beer mats.

Billy I don't usually do that sort of thing.

Pat I could see that. As fan dances go, yours left a lot to be desired.

Billy But how did I get into that state?

Pat Well, you know how it is at stag parties. Some fool starts pouring shorts into peoples drinks and some unsuspecting idiot gets sozzled.

Billy And I was the unsuspecting idiot?

Pat That's right.

Billy What happened next?

Pat Well, by closing time everyone was fine and merry with you leading the race to drink the pub dry. The landlord shouted "Time" and you said—(*in a mock drunken accent*)—"Letsh go back to my plashe", so we did.

Billy I see. That explains the party. I suppose I flaked out and a couple of blokes put me to bed.

Pat Right on the first count, wrong on the second.

Billy But how . . .?

Pat You collapsed all right. On here—(*indicating the sofa*)—so we left you. When everyone had gone *I* got you to your feet and put you to bed

Billy That's very good of you. I very much appreciate that but now I must get dressed. I'm expecting some visitors today and I must look respectable. (*He gets up and goes to the bedroom but returns immediately. He stops, looks inside his sheet and gasps in horror, clutching the sheet tightly to his body*)

Billy I've got nothing on under this sheet!

Pat Are you trying to turn me on?

Billy Certainly not! Don't you understand? Beneath this sheet I am absolutely naked.

Pat What you mean is that at this moment you are impersonating a cross between Lady Godiva and Lawrence of Arabia.

Billy This is no time for silly jokes. Last night you stripped me naked . . .

Pat As the day you were born!

Billy Probably feasted your eyes on my defenceless nudity . . .

Pat Do me a favour. I've seen more naked blokes than you've eaten tins of beans.

Billy What! What the hell are you?

Pat A nurse.

Billy Oh, I'm sorry.

Pat At the mental home.

Billy Eh?

Pat It's all right. Don't worry. I don't spend my leisure hours looking for schizophrenics who think they're the Sheik of Araby. (*Flicking his sheet*) Mind you, you'll find yourself a suitable case for treatment if you don't calm down a bit. Now go back to your bedroom. You'll find your clothes neatly folded on the chair by the window. (*Moving to the sliding cupboard and opening it*) I hung your trousers in here. (*She gets them out*) Here. (*Passing the trousers*) Now go and get dressed.

Billy (*taking the trousers*) Thanks. (*He goes to the bedroom and continues talking*) Look, are you sure you didn't take advantage of me last night? It is important you know.

Pat No I did not, you soft idiot. Now hurry up and get dressed.

Billy comes from the bedroom in his underpants with his clothes in his arms

Billy Then why are you dressed like that?

Pat Don't you mean why am I *un*dressed like that? It's quite simple really. As I said before, that was quite a wild party you threw last night.

Billy (*continuing to dress*) I'm sorry I missed it.

Pat Well one thing led to another. Someone put this record on and bet I wouldn't strip to it. He was a cocky devil, you know the sort, always trying to say things to shock someone so I thought "Right, Buster, now you've met your match", and I called his bluff.

Billy How?

Pat I said, "Okay, I will if you will". Well, he had no choice, had he?

Billy (*exploding*) Do you mean to say that while I lay blotto on my sofa, naked men and women were cavorting in an orgy of wild ecstasy all around me?

Pat Hardly. He was stalling by the time he reached his string vest, but when he got to his Y-fronts he began to look wildly around for a means of avoiding embarrassment. Fortunately for him, and me, help was at hand.

Billy How?

Pat One of his mates turned the record off.

Billy So all we have to do is find the record, play it backwards for you to put your clothes back on and you can leave.

Pat I'm afraid it won't be as easy as that.

Billy No, I didn't think it would be. Why not?

Pat When everyone had gone and I'd put you to bed, I discovered my clothes were nowhere to be found. I presume that idiot I made a fool of had run off with them as a kind of revenge.

Billy Oh that's marvellous. Yes, that's great. That is absolutely perfect. Super. Just what I needed.

Pat Now what's the matter?

Billy Look—um ...

Pat Pat.

Billy Pat, there's something I've got to tell you.

Pat I know, you're the son of Jack the Ripper and now you're going to chop me into pieces and throw me into the alley way.

Billy For goodness' sake!

Pat Okay. I'm sorry. What should I know?

Billy Perhaps I should start at the beginning.

Pat Please do.

Billy Well, to start with I never knew my dad. He and Mum weren't married.

Pat You mean that you're a ...

Billy Yes.

Pat Well, that's nothing to be upset about.

Billy Oh, that doesn't bother me. When it was announced that a stork was nesting on Mum's roof you can guess what happened.

Pat Dad scarpered?

Billy Quicker than a Protestant going through Dublin. No-one ever saw hide nor hair of him again.

Pat Which left you and Mum?

Billy And Aunty Ethel.

Pat Aunty Ethel?

Billy Aunty Ethel. Aunty Ethel doted on me. She used to call me her little Willy. I suppose she felt sorry for me. Anyway, when Aunty Ethel died she left me all her wordly goods.

Pat A carved what-not, some jewellery that had sentimental value and her Post Office savings account.

Billy On the contrary! Aunty Ethel died a very rich woman—much to everyone's surprise—and left me a considerable sum of money.

Pat (*looking around*) Which explains why you're living in such splendour. *Now.*

Billy That's the point. There was a clause in the conditions of the legacy.

Pat There always is.

Billy I could have the money when I reached the age of twenty-one.

Pat Which is today—happy birthday.

Billy So long as I remained pure until that time.

Pat Pure?

Billy Yes, you know. She didn't want me getting up to the same mischief as Mum and Dad had.

Pat Well, I still don't see what you were getting so uptight about.

Billy Look. If someone calls and sees us here, with you dressed like that, they are not going to think the night before my twenty-first birthday was a very pure one are they?

Pat That's terrible.

Billy I know.

Pat So what would happen to the money?

Billy It would all go to my mother on my twenty-first.

Pat Is that so bad?

Billy It's very bad. If Mum gets her hands on that money I'll not see a penny of it.

Pat Doesn't she deserve it after struggling all those years to bring you up?

Billy She didn't bring me up! She contested the will when Aunty Ethel died but it didn't get far. When she knew she was fighting a losing game she practically disowned me. I spent my childhood with various long lost relatives who weren't very pleased at being found when they discovered it was their turn to look after me.

Pat I understand how you feel. Now, no-one must know I stayed here last night.

Billy Right.

The phone rings. Billy answers it.

(*On the phone*) Hello. . . . Yes, that's me. . . . Today. . . . Yes. . . . Right away?? . . . I see, thank you. (*He puts down the phone*) Oh hell!

Pat What's the matter?

Billy That was the solicitor's secretary. A solicitor is on his way to discuss the legacy.

Pat And I'm still here.

Billy With no clothes on and he'll be here very soon.

There is a knock at the door

I didn't think he'd be that quick! You'll have to hide.

Pat hides in the kitchen area. Billy opens the door.

Nigel, a telegram boy is standing there. He is a cheeky-looking fellow—roughly the same size as Pat

Nigel Morning, sir. Telegram for Mr William Nelson.

Billy That's me. (*He takes the telegram*)

Nigel (*holding out a notebook*) If you wouldn't mind signing here, sir, just to say you've received it.

Billy Do you have a pen?

Nigel Sorry, I haven't, sir.

Billy Oh, well step inside while I look for one.

Nigel steps in and closes the door

Nigel Had quite a party last night, sir.

Billy Yes. I—er—believe I did. (*Looking for a pen*) Now, where did I put that . . . Are you sure you haven't got a pen?

Nigel Positive sir. Sorry and all that.

Billy Let me look in the bedroom.

Nigel Sobered up now have you, sir?

Billy Yes. Just about.

Billy goes into the bedroom

Nigel sits on the sofa

Nigel Mind you. You were in a hell of a state sir. What with the fan-dancing down at the pub, and then bringing us all back here.

Billy emerges slowly from bedroom, wonderment on his face

I'm not surprised you keeled over on the sofa.

Billy You were here last night?

Nigel That's right sir. We started off at the *Pear Tree* on me mate's stag night then we ended up here. A right do it was too. There was some bird here, a right little raver I reckon, an I bet she wouldn't strip to this record. You'll never believe what she said.

Billy Try me.

Nigel She said, "Only if you will". Cheeky madam. Well, it didn't go too far. One of me mates turned the record off, thank God. I don't mind telling you, sir, she fair put the wind up me. It'll make me think twice before I suggest anything like that again. Mind you, I got my own back. I nicked all her clothes and hid 'em in me mate's car.

*During the above Billy moves and stands furiously above Nigel, who is totally
unaware*

I wonder where she stayed last night?

Billy (*pouncing on Nigel and dragging him to his feet*) You snivelling little
runt!

Nigel Hey! hang on a minute!

Billy I've half a mind to throw you down the stairs.

Nigel (*shaking himself free*) Wait a minute, guv'nor.

Billy Don't you tell me to wait a minute, you obnoxious little swine.

Nigel What have I done?

Billy What have you done? Lost me sixty thousand quid, that's what.

Nigel What! I never touched any bleedin' money. Gordon Bennett!

Billy You miserable slob! I'll teach you . . .

Nigel Help!

Billy is about to hit Nigel as Pat appears

Pat Billy!

Billy stops, calms down and walks away

That isn't going to get us anywhere, is it?

Nigel Oh blimey. It's her!

Pat Yes. It's me.

Nigel Did you stay here all night?

Pat Yes.

Nigel (*to Billy*) Well, I did you a favour then, didn't I?

Billy (*angered again*) I swear I'll break you into tiny pieces . . .

Nigel (*backing away*) Call him off.

Pat Billy!

Billy Oh hell, what are we going to do?

Nigel Look, I'm sorry if I've upset someone . . .

Billy Upset someone?

Nigel But would you mind explaining what's going on? I don't know what
I've done, but if there's anything I can do to make amends, then I will.

Pat Sit down and I'll explain.

Nigel sits

Have a drink. (*She gives him the glass that she and Billy emptied their
glasses into earlier*)

Nigel Thanks. (*He drinks and chokes*) Blimey, sir, what's in here?

Billy Poison with a bit of luck.

Pat looks at Billy menacingly

Okay—sorry.

Nigel takes another drink

Nigel This isn't so bad after all. (*He takes another drink*) Have you got
any more? (*He looks around, finds a bottle and helps himself*)

Billy Thirsty, are you?

Nigel (*ignoring Billy*) Right then, darling, you were about to tell me where I went wrong in playing Cupid between you and birthday boy over there.

Pat If you carry on provoking him he'll be quite justified in clocking you.

Nigel Okay, okay, okay. (*He pours another drink*) Not another word. Now fill me in.

Billy looks up

With the story, I mean.

Pat It's quite simple really. Billy here is twenty-one today.

Nigel raises his glass and drinks

Now, if he has remained pure until his twenty-first birthday . . .

Nigel How do you mean—pure?

Pat Well, if he hasn't—er . . .

Pat whispers in Nigel's ear. He grins

He stands to inherit a very large legacy.

Nigel The sixty thousand quid he was screaming about?

Pat That's right.

Nigel So until I put my foot in it last night, he was a . . .

Billy (*angrily*) I still am.

Nigel Blimey. Twenty-one and never . . . (*He whistles and pours another drink*) Well, guv'nor—(*raising his glass*)—what you never had you never missed.

Billy rises, Pat pushes him down again

Hang on a minute. If he's still—pure?

Pat nods

What's all the bother about?

Pat The solicitor is due here at any moment.

Nigel So?

Pat Take a look around and what do you see?

Nigel The remains of a party.

Pat Go on.

Nigel The man of the house looking as though he's been caught with his trousers down.

Pat M—m—m.

Nigel And you in a state of undress.

Pat What will the solicitor think?

Nigel The same as me I suppose. That you and he have been . . . (*Realization dawns*) Oh hell.

Billy (*clapping*) Oh well done, mastermind. You've worked it out.

Nigel (*pouring another drink*) Well what can I do to help?

Billy Why don't you have a drink while you think about it.

Nigel Oh, thanks. (*He looks at his full glass, looks at Billy and shrugs*) Why don't you just go home before Rumpole of the Bailey turns up?

Pat I can't, can I? Your mate is driving around with my clothes in his car.

Nigel Can't you just hide?

Billy No, too risky in a small place like this.

Nigel (*sitting*) You've got a bit of a problem on your hands here, squire.

Pat Don't you mean *we've* got a bit of a problem? You're in this with us. If you hadn't been so clever last night this poor innocent boy would be on his way to a fortune by now.

Nigel I feel sorry about that. I know how he feels, it ain't easy without a bit of the ready. Me and the girl friend are thinking of emigrating. It's supposed to be easier to get a bit of loot together on the other side of the world.

Billy (*sorely*) Well, when you've scraped together your first sixty thousand, perhaps you'll send it over to make-up for this.

Nigel No, no, no there must be some way out of this. (*He stands*) Blimey, I don't half feel queer.

Billy Perhaps it's something you ate.

Nigel Yeh. (*Taking another drink*) Now let me think.

Billy Again?

Nigel Now hang on. Let's get this right. (*To Pat*) You've got to stay here?

Pat Right.

Nigel Your solicitor will see her?

Billy Right.

Nigel Then the solicitor mustn't know she's a woman.

Billy Oh my God, the man's an idiot. What am I going to do. Pass her off as a hatstand? (*He gets up and talks to imaginary solicitor*) Good morning, Mr Solicitor, do come in. Hang your coat over here. Woman? No this isn't a woman this is where you hang your coat. Pardon? It looks like a woman. Oh, does it? I can't say I'd noticed. You see, having remained pure all my life I wouldn't know . . . (*He flops back into his ckair*) No. A nice try but it wouldn't work.

Nigel No, you don't understand. Just don't tell him she's a woman.

Billy No, he'll know.

Nigel No he won't. Not if she's dressed as a bloke.

There is a silence as the suggestion sinks in

Pat That's the best suggestion yet, but I can't get his clothes on. I tried last night when I wanted to go home.

They sit despondently

Billy Even so that's not a bad idea. (*He collects another bottle and pours Nigel a drink*)

Nigel Thanks. (*He drinks*) What she needs is some clothes from a bloke the same size as her.

Billy helps him lift his glass

Billy (*pouring another drink*) Jolly good idea.

Nigel (*obviously getting drunk*) It's got to be a bloke who's already here.

Billy And it can't be me.

Nigel No. Because the slister's coming to see you. (*He is now slurring his words*) And you're the wrong size. (*He wags his finger at Billy*)

Billy (*pouring another drink*) Now I wonder if there are any other men here?

Nigel clumsily finishes his drink, sits thinking, then suddenly jumps up

Nigel Yes. There's me.

Billy has to hold Nigel up

Billy Steady now. Let's just see if your jacket fits.

Pat and Billy remove Nigel's jacket and drape it over the back of the sofa

Pat It ought to fit.

There is a knock at the door

Billy Oh my God that'll be him.
Pat Tell him to wait.

Billy runs to the door and opens it

> *The solicitor, Mr Shoesmith, is standing at the door, briefcase in hand*

Shoesmith Good morning. I am . . .
Billy Sorry, you'll have to wait. (*He shuts the door*)
Pat Shall I hide?
Billy I think you'd better—in the bedroom, quick!

> *Pat runs to the bedroom. There is a knock on the door. Billy opens the door*

Shoesmith Ah, good morning. I am . . .
Billy (*shutting the door again*) Ah-h-h . . . Pat, help.
Pat (*appearing from the bedroom*) What's the matter?
Billy (*pointing to Nigel*) What about him?
Pat Do you think he'll see him?
Billy With that much drink inside him, he'll *smell* him! Come on, in the kitchen.

Between them they move the limp and unco-ordinated Nigel to the kitchen area. He is propped up and the curtain closed

> Right. Back in the bedroom.

> *Pat exits to the bedroom*

There is a knock at the door. Billy is half-way to the door as the phone rings. He looks backwards and forwards, between phone and door—confused. He rushes to the phone and picks it up

> (*On the phone*) Clear off! Can't you see we're busy? (*He slams the phone down and goes to the front door. He opens it*)

Shoesmith Good morning . . .

There is a pause

> Aren't you going to shut the door?
Billy Not until you're inside. Do come in.

Mr Shoesmith darts inside

Shoesmith Right, you can close it now.

Billy Are you all right?

Shoesmith Yes, Yes quite, thank you.

Billy You look a little on edge, can I offer you a drink?

Shoesmith Well, I shouldn't. But as you are the only client I am meeting today, why not? Let's treat it as a premature celebratory drink eh? A small Scotch if I may, with ice.

Billy I'm sorry, there's no ice. Will water do? There's no difference, anyway.

Shoesmith I'm not sure if the captain of the *Titanic* would agree with you there, but water will be fine.

Billy sidles into the kitchen without opening the curtain—a difficult operation —and returns with a milk bottle of water

Billy Now . . . (*Searching through bottles*) Whisky with a little *cold* water wasn't it?

Billy finds a whisky bottle, but it is empty. Mr Shoesmith sorts through papers in his briefcase. Billy picks up different glasses, sniffing each one in turn. He finds one containing whisky and carefully pours it into the whisky bottle. He turns and proudly gives the empty glass to Mr Shoesmith

Here we go. (*He pours the whisky back into the glass*) And water. (*He pours from the milk bottle*)

Shoesmith Thank you. (*Raising his glass*) Here's to a smooth transaction. (*He drinks and pulls a face*) Smoother than that, anyway.

Billy I presume you have called about my inheritance?

Shoesmith Yes, I represent Jackson, Jackson, Jackson, Jackson and Jones, and before you ask—(*laughing*)—No, I am not Mr Jackson.

Billy Then you must be Mr Jones.

Shoesmith Good gracious no! He's dead. I'm simply a junior member of the company. My name is Shoesmith. Rodney Shoesmith. I have only recently joined Jackson, Jackson, Jackson, Jackson and Jones. I usually deal in house conveyancing, so this kind of thing is new to me.

Billy Well, it's new to me as well—so don't expect me to help you. You're supposed to be the legal expert.

Shoesmith Quite. Now let's get down to business.

Pat appears in the bedroom door and signs to Billy that she does not have the jacket

Shoesmith does not see Pat. Billy makes wild signs with his arms for her to get out of sight. Shoesmith notices him, and frowns

Pat disappears

Billy Missed it again. (*Laughing nervously*) This place is infested with flies. (*He collects the jacket from the sofa, sidles across to the bedroom door and hurls it in, shutting the door smartly and breathing a sigh of relief*).

Shoesmith Firstly we have to establish that you are indeed Mr William Nelson—(*consulting documents*)—who was born in Shrewsbury Royal Infirmary in nineteen fifty-six.

Billy Well, I have my birth certificate.

Shoesmith That should suffice. But of course, you may be an impostor who has gained possession of Mr Nelson's birth certificate.

Billy Passport?

Shoesmith You've been abroad?

Billy No, but I thought I might go if I came into some money.

Shoesmith So you have begun making preparations, eh? Good fellow. Now, if you would let me see your passport and birth certificate we can start moving and, with a bit of luck, you will be a richer man.

Billy Right. I'll fetch them for you. (*He goes to the bedroom and returns with a large brown envelope*)

Mr Shoesmith sorts through his papers

Here you are.

Shoesmith Thank you.

The drunken Nigel appears from behind the kitchen, in a daze. Billy leaps up, grabs a bottle, gives it to Nigel and ushers him back behind kitchen curtain

So you come from Shrewsbury, do you? (*Looking at documents and making notes*) An old Salopian. I remember when I was a junior clerk I stayed in Shrewsbury for a short time. I was working then for a firm of solicitors who dealt mainly with agricultural transactions. A large private farm was being sold off in separate lots. Yes, I remember it all now. Three weeks we were there, at the *Green Dragon* hotel, all expenses paid. I really thought I was the cat's whiskers; a hotel room and an expense account. I don't mind telling you, young lad, that some extra wild oats were scattered around Shropshire that year.

Billy I don't remember much about Shrewsbury, I left there when I was five. Are those in order?

Shoesmith I'll just check. Let's see, passport first. If her Britannic Majesty says you're William Nelson, who am I to argue? Now, birth certificate —(*opening it up*)—oh, I see it says "Father unknown".

Billy Yes, you see I am the result of what you might call a "hit and run".

Shoesmith And your father did the running?

Billy Yes.

Shoesmith The swine.

Billy I think Mum said something like that.

Shoesmith Well, those are fine. (*Handing back the passport and birth certificate*) If you would be kind enough to sign these forms we can move to the next, more delicate area of the legacy. (*He hands Billy two forms*)

Billy (*quickly reading the forms*) No, I couldn't possibly sign those.

Shoesmith But my dear boy, you must!

Billy I don't think I should, you know.

Shoesmith What possible reason could you have for not signing them?

Billy They are an agreement to sell my house, and I don't have one.

Shoesmith I'm so sorry. As I said, house conveyancing is my usual area. I must have left the other forms in the car. If you will excuse me for a moment, I must go and get them.

Billy Mr Shoesmith, you mentioned the next, more delicate area of the legacy.

Shoesmith Yes.

Billy How exactly do I set about proving my purity?

Shoesmith Quite simply, really. A sworn statement from you, a thorough examination of your home by a police officer for tell-tale signs of having hanky-panky, and a medical examination just to make sure.

Billy And that's it?

Shoesmith Together with any response from our advertisement, yes.

Billy Advertisement?

Shoesmith Oh yes, it's standard proceedure. (*He produces a clipping from his briefcase and hands it to Billy*) This advertisement was placed in *The Times*, the *Standard* and the *Gazette*. (*He puts down his spectacles and stands*) Perhaps you would cast an eye over it while I pop down to the car for the other forms. I won't be long.

Billy Hey—hang on, this is under a section headed Property for Sale.

Shoesmith Yes. I'm sorry about that, I normally deal in conveyancing. Did you know?

Billy Yes. You did mention it.

Shoesmith Shan't be a moment.

Shoesmith goes

Billy (*to himself, looking at the clipping*) Look at this—only twenty-one, and here I am, stuck between a desirable end-terrace and a three-bed semi-det. with mod. cons.

Pat comes from the bedroom

Pat Well, come on then! Let's move.

Billy Oh blimey, I forgot about that.

They draw back the curtain to find Nigel standing erect, staring into oblivion with a stupid, fixed grin

Pat Oh my God, it's the original *rigor mortis*.

Billy Ha, ha, smile, you're on Candid Camera.

Pat (*waving her hand in front of Nigel's eyes*) He's out cold, you know.

Billy Never mind about that, let's get the rest of his clothes off for a start.

With difficulty, they manoeuvre the stiff, drunken Nigel to a chair where they manage, again with difficulty, to take off his shirt, trousers and shoes. Nigel mumbles all the time

Pat What are we going to do with him?

Billy Well he *could* be passed off as a hatstand. He's stiff enough.

Pat Don't be stupid. You'll have to sober him up somehow.

Billy I know! Hot black coffee.

Pat You haven't got time, get a bowl of water.

Billy does so, while Pat slaps Nigel repeatedly across the face

Billy What are you doing? I know it's all his fault, but it's a bit below the belt to hit the poor fellow when he's in that state.

Pat I'm trying to get some life back into him.

Billy Looks as though you're knocking it out of him. Anyway, don't tell me you weren't enjoying that. The look on your face was pure bliss.

Pat All right, perhaps I was killing two birds but we must get this fellow mobile. Now, up on his feet for starters.

Billy puts the bowl of water on the table and they stand Nigel up

Get him walking.

They kick, push and pull Nigel around the room

Now let's make him run.

They manage to do so

Faster!

They go faster

Stop!

Pat slaps Nigel again

Nigel OW!

Billy (*in a mock-spaceman voice*) We have contact!

Pat Let's keep it then. Shake him up!

Billy grasps Nigel's shoulders and violently shakes him backwards and forwards. Pat gets the bowl of water

Okay. Stop! Right sit him down.

Billy You've practically beaten him to a pulp. Now what are you going to do? Drown him?

Pat Hardly.

Billy You're not giving him a wash?

Pat Hold the bowl in front of him.

Pat slaps Nigel's face again

Nigel OW!

As he shouts, Pat pushes his head into the water

Pat One, two, three, four. (*She pulls him out*)

Nigel Bloody hell!

She repeats the process

Try that again and I'll . . .

Pat slaps him once more. He is silenced

Pat Be quiet. You are now sober.

Billy Have you finished?

Pat Certainly, he's as sober as he needs to be. (*She picks up the bowl and takes it to the kitchen*)

Billy Well, that's some way to sober a bloke up. Where did you learn that trick?

Pat It's all part of my training at the hospital. Drunkenness is very similar to a disorder of the mind known as a Cerebral Comatose Malorder or mild senility. Patients, for a short time can be given a set of shock treatments which increases the awareness and response to any suggestions directed at them.

Billy Pardon?

Pat He's not really sober, I shocked him into thinking he is. He will now do what you want without question.

Billy Eh?

Pat The thinking part of his brain is still pickling in Vat Sixty-nine. The shock treatment has bypassed that, so . . .

Billy Whatever I say—he will do?

Pat For pity's sake . . .

Billy Stand.

Nigel stands

Pat Don't start mucking about . . .

Billy Sit.

Nigel sits

Pat You are in control of a human being . . .

Billy What is your name?

Pat That is a lot of responsibility . . .

Nigel Nigel.

Billy Say "sir" when you speak to me!

Pat And it could cost me my job if anyone found out I'd been doing this.

Nigel Nigel, sir!

Billy Hey, this is great!

Pat You haven't listened to a word I've said. You! (*Pointing to Nigel*) Tell him what I said.

Nigel The thinking part of my brain is still pickling in Vat Sixty-nine so for pity's sake don't start mucking about. You are in control of a human being. That is a lot of responsibility and it could cost her her job if anyone found out she'd been doing this.

Pat Straight from the horse's mouth.

Nigel I am not a horse.

Billy I thought you said he wasn't thinking.

Pat You don't have to think to know you're not a horse. Have you taken in what I said.

Billy Yes. You're right of course. I'll be very careful.

There is a knock at the door

Pat That's him now, I'll get this lot on.

Pat grabs the clothes and runs to the bedroom. As she goes, she spots the solicitor's glasses and grabs those as well

Billy Who is it?

Shoesmith (*off*) It's me, Shoesmith.

Billy Wait a minute. (*He composes himself, swallows hard*) Nigel, you are my neighbour.

Shoesmith (*off*) Come along. (*He knocks again*) We're not going to go through all this again, are we?

Billy Who are you?

Nigel I am your neighbour.

Billy Great stuff! (*He opens the door*)

Shoesmith enters

Shoesmith I'm sorry about that. Very absent minded of . . . (*He sees Nigel*) My God. Who's this?

Billy Er—this is Nigel, who lives in the flat across the landing.

Shoesmith Then what is he doing here?

Billy I am examining him.

Shoesmith What for?

Billy Er—I don't know.

Shoesmith Then what do you hope to find?

Billy Um—not a lot.

Shoesmith Look, what is going on?

Billy Nigel was having a shave, having just got up, when he thought he noticed a rash, on his back.

Shoesmith On his back? How did he see that?

Billy In the mirror.

Shoesmith (*incredulously*) He was shaving with his back to the mirror?

Billy No. He has two mirrors. On opposite walls. He has lots of mirrors, all over the place. He likes looking at himself—all over.

Shoesmith Disgusting. (*To Nigel*) What are you, some kind of Nancy Boy?

Nigel I am his neighbour. I am not a horse.

Shoesmith looks puzzled

Shoesmith I think you are an idiot. (*To Billy*) Did you find a rash?

Billy No he seems to be all right.

Shoesmith Then you may leave us to our private business. Go home, young man.

Nigel stands and walks towards the door. Billy guides him in a circle back to his seat

Billy I don't think that's such a good idea. I think we should let him stay for a while. (*Trying to think*) We can't be too sure can we? I mean—he might be struck ill at any moment. He could have anything, couldn't he?

Shoesmith About the only thing he's likely to have is a severe case of alcoholic poisoning by the smell of him. What do you shave with, Johnny Walker? (*He looks round*)

Nigel I shave with . . .

Shoesmith (*looking around*) Oh do be quiet! (*To Billy*) Have you seen my spectacles?

Billy No.

Shoesmith (*searching all the time*) I'm sure I had them when I first came. (*To Nigel*) Have you got them?

Nigel No.

Billy Are you sure you had them when you came?

Shoesmith Of course I am. I can't read or write a thing without them. We wouldn't have completed our transactions if I couldn't see.

Billy But we didn't complete them. You gave me the wrong forms—remember?

Shoesmith (*worried*) Then how did I drive here without my glasses?

Billy I don't know.

Shoesmith (*sitting shakily*) Do you think I might have another drink? I'm beginning to crack up, I'm sure of it.

Billy roots amongst the bottles

My horoscope said that today I should look out for unexpected surprises. I remember thinking "How can it be unexpected if you're looking out for it?" Well, I wasn't expecting this. They should have left me with the property conveyances. This isn't my area.

Billy gives him a drink

Thank you. (*He swallows it in one go*) What am I going to do?

Billy Look, just calm down. You've mislaid your glasses, that's all. Do you have a spare pair?

Shoesmith Yes, at home.

Billy Then leave everything here. Take a pleasant stroll home.

Shoesmith A pleasant stroll? I live twenty-five miles away.

Billy Well you can't drive, can you?

Shoesmith I could take a train.

Billy Marvellous. Take a train home, have lunch with your wife . . .

Shoesmith I'm not married.

Billy Have a quiet lunch, collect your spare specs and catch the train back. I'll still be here and we can finish off the work.

Shoesmith (*much calmer*) That seems to be a sound suggestion. (*He stands*) I'll be back as soon as I can.

Billy opens the door, Mr Shoesmith reaches the door, then stops, turns sharply and addresses Nigel in a lecturing manner

Now look here, young man. The time has come for you to realize that there is no place in this world for people like you. We are strong, upright citizens trying to lead responsible lives without blemish. We know about your sort with your two-way mirrors, your lace cuffs, your flowery shirts, your tightly tailored trousers and your all-over body talc.

Oh yes, we know, and we are disgusted! Well it's got to stop, do you understand? We don't want you perverting pure young men like this. When I return, I don't want to find you here, do you understand?

Nigel I understand.

Shoesmith Good. (*To Billy*) I shall be as quick as possible but I don't expect to be back until late afternoon.

Billy That's all right, take your time. Good-bye.

Shoesmith Good-bye.

Shoesmith goes

Billy Phew. (*He sits on the sofa, exhausted*)

Pat appears in the doorway dressed in Nigel's outfit

Pat Telegram, sir?

Billy Uh. (*He jumps*) I forgot about you.

Pat Thank you. What was all the shouting about?

Billy Shoesmith.

Pat Who?

Billy Shoesmith, the solicitor, he was giving Nigel a ticking off.

Pat Why?

Billy He thinks he's gay.

Pat What! Why?

Billy It's too difficult to explain now.

Pat If I tried to explain *anything* that's happened this morning, I'd find it difficult. Jeepers, what a mess!

Billy Just as a matter of interest, why are you helping me? You're putting yourself in a pretty precarious position purely for me. Is there any reason?

Pat No, not really. I suppose it's the kind of person I am. I care about people—particularly the underdog or the guy who's having all the hard luck. When a fellow slips on a banana skin, everyone laughs. Then what happens? We all walk away laughing. No-one stops to help the chap up or see if he's hurt.

Billy Except you?

Pat Okay, if that's the way it looks. I mean, I don't go out of my way to look for victims of society, but when an occasion arises, I do stop and consider people's feelings. We are, after all, human beings here to live and love together.

Billy Which is why you took the job you did?

Pat I don't think it's as corny as that, although there's probably some truth in it.

Billy You mean you just don't like to see people being kicked when they are down?

Pat Or not being given a chance to defend themselves because of other people's stupidity, or having to resort to collusion to get what is rightfully theirs. If only we could all respect each other for what we are. I mean, "What a piece of work is a man! How noble in reason! . . . In form, in moving, how express and admirable!"

There is a silence as Billy digests this

Billy (*with a whistle*) Do you really think that?

Pat Sure. But I couldn't have said it without some help from Shakespeare. Comes from *Hamlet*, that does. I learnt it at school and it's always meant something to me. (*Ponderously*) William Shakespeare—hey! I wonder if his mates called *him* Billy?

Billy Who cares? What do we do now? We've got rid of Shoesmith for a few hours so we should be able to get everything sorted out by the time he returns.

Pat I think we ought to see about sorting out your flat for a start. I made your bed while I was imprisoned in there—(*Nodding to the bedroom*)— but there's a bit more squaring up to be done, so I'll get on with that while you dispose of the bottles!

Billy What shall I do with them?

Pat Have you got a box?

Billy Yes, there's my grocery delivery.

Pat Well, take your groceries out and put the bottles in.

Pat goes to the bedroom

Billy, in the alcove, takes three catering-size tins of baked beans, instant mash and creamed rice from the box and puts them on a shelf. He then takes a tin of Andrews and puts that on the shelf checking them as he does so

Billy Let's see, beans m-hm, instant mash, y-es, creamed rice and Andrews. All here. Good.

Pat returns

Pat (*standing in the bedroom door*) By the way . . .

Billy Yes?

Pat What was the telegram about?

Billy Telegram? What? I didn't—I mean . . .

Pat Haven't you read it?

Billy Not yet, no.

Pat Well, read it now.

Billy searches and eventually finds the telegram. He frantically rips it open and reads it

Billy Oh hell! (*He sits, deflated*)

Pat What does it say?

Billy holds it out, she takes it and reads

"Happy Birthday, darling. Stop. Will see you on Saturday with lovely surprise. Stop. Love Mummy. Stop."

Billy (*resigned*) The vulture has spread her wings and at this moment is diving down on her prey.

Pat Don't let her win now, Billy boy. You've managed it this far.

Billy Okay. Let's get rid of these bottles.

They both put the bottles in the box and take it to the kitchen area

And try and think of something to do with him. For how long will he
do as he's told?

Pat Until the drunkenness wears off.

Billy That should be okay.

Pat I know just the place for him. (*She opens the sliding cupboard door*)
Nigel, stand up, please.

Nigel stands up

Come here.

Nigel goes to her

When I clap my hands you will step into this cupboard and stand still
and lifeless. (*She claps*)

Nigel goes into the cupboard. She closes the door

There you are. (*She looks around*) The old place looks presentable now.

Billy And I feel ready to face that old Meadow Lady called Mother.
(*Picking up bottles*) I'll just take this box of bottles down to the bin and
then we'll be ready to do battle.

Pat The telegram said she had a "lovely surprise" and was signed "Love,
Mummy". You don't think she's turned over a new leaf, do you?

Billy No! You don't turn new leaves over when you're raking muck.
And that's all she's ever done. (*Going to the door*) Open this for me.

Pat opens the door

Thanks. Won't be long.

*Billy goes out. Pat looks around, tidies up records, etc., picks up several
items and takes them off into the bedroom*

Mum (*off*) Come on, pick your feet up!

We hear two people clumping along outside

If there's another flight of stairs I'll scream. 'Ere we are.

*Mum appears at the doorway. She is blowsy. She is accompanied by
Annie, a shy, ultra-plain, bespectacled young woman who wears a long
straight coat, a beret and carries an old brown suitcase. Mum knocks*

Billy? Coo-ee! (*To Annie*) Now remember, be nice. (*Calling*) Billy
darling!

Pat appears from the bedroom

Excuse me, does Mr William Nelson live here?

Pat (*coughing and coaxing a deep voice*) Yes.

Mum enters the room and looks around. Annie follows and stands near her

Mum Then where is he?

Pat I—I don't know.

Mum Is that his bedroom?
Pat Yes.
Mum What are you doing in there?
Pat Looking for him.
Mum To give him a telegram, I hope?
Pat (*indignantly*) Yes.
Mum (*to Annie*) That'll be the one I sent him. He isn't even expecting me yet. (*She spots the opened telegram*) Is that the telegram?
Pat Yes.
Mum But it's been opened!
Pat Er, yes.
Mum This is highly irregular, young man. Give me your number. I intend to report you after lunch.
Pat Oh no, ma'am. We always open telegrams now. Part of the new streamlined service. We open 'em, read 'em, an' if it's bad news, rip 'em up! That way the telegram department can never be accused of bearing sad tidings. Good for the public image, y'see. All part of the service. As Busby says, must fly now! "Toodle oo".

Pat leaves, quickly

Mum (*staring after him*) Cheeky little sod!

Mum walks to the sofa and sits. Annie follows

We'll just sit here and wait for him to turn up. Now remember, young Annie. We've got to get him falling in love with you. With a bit of luck you'll be married in two months. You'll be Mrs William Nelson, sixty thousand quid better off, and living in style with your new housekeeper —me—living in. Now, you know what to do?
Annie (*in a voice as plain as her appearance*) Be coy but polite, laugh at his jokes, catch his eye whenever I can, but always play hard to get.
Mum That's it. It always works. Especially the last bit.

They sit in silence

Billy appears in the doorway. He has obviously rushed but slows down. He shows no surprise at seeing them. He looks at them, they cannot see him. He grins and takes an imaginary bow and arrow and shoots them. He then shoots them with pistols, taking careful aim, etc., a sten gun, and finally tosses hand-grenades. Having satisfied himself he goes out of sight and immediately starts singing and whistling

That's him. (*She gets up and goes to the door*)

Billy appears

Mum stretches out her arms to meet him

Billy!

The Lights fade to a Black-out, and—

the CURTAIN *falls*

ACT II

The same. Immediately following

Billy has just entered the room

Mum Billy!

Billy Mother, you again.

Mum Again? I last saw you three years ago.

Billy That's what I mean.

Mum (*endearingly*) Oh Billy.

Billy (*mockingly*) Oh Mother.

Mum Oh Billy.

Billy Oh shut up!

Mum Aren't you glad to see your mother's back?

Billy I will be. (*Pointing*) There's the door.

Mum Oh Billy.

Billy Don't start that again. Look, Mother, I've got a pretty shrewd idea why you're here and it's not going to work. I've given up a lot over the last few years to satisfy the demands of Aunty Ethel, and I think I justly deserve the rewards.

Mum Billy, I've just come to see you.

Billy And to make a last ditch stand to get your hands on the legacy. Well let me tell you—Mother dear—it's no use so you may as well leave. (*He points to the door*)

Mum No, Billy darling, you've got it all wrong.

Billy Don't you think it's a bit late to start calling me "Billy darling"? For the last twenty-one years I've been the snivelling little brat who had the misfortune and bad judgement to pop out and claim you as my mother.

Mum It wasn't my fault . . .

Billy Well, it wasn't mine, was it. Over the years you've blamed me for a lot of things although I don't really see why, I was never closer than a train journey from you, but my birth is one thing you *cannot* blame me for.

Mum It was an accident.

Billy Oh, an accident, was it? I'm sorry; I didn't know. Let me apologize straight away. "Mother, I'm terribly sorry I was born. I promise I won't do it again."

Mum No, I don't mean that. What I mean is, the bit before shouldn't have happened.

Billy For once in my life, I find myself agreeing with you.

Mum It was your father's fault.

Billy Bound to be. I suppose you had nothing to do with it? I don't suppose you were even there.

Mum Of course I was. I was working as a chambermaid in one of the hotels. There were a lot of people staying in the building at the time.

Billy I can believe that. People do stay in hotels.

Mum Some of them were men.

Billy Yes. I can believe that too. I've noticed that some people *are* men.

Mum I was turning down the sheets.

Billy For the men?

Mum For everyone. That's how it happened.

Billy I think, Mother, that my conception entailed a little more than simply turning down the sheets, although you do seem to be in the right room.

Mum No, I mean the power cut.

Billy Power cut?

Mum Yes. It was quite late and I was going from room to room . . .

Billy Turning down sheets?

Mum Exactly. I got to this particular room, knocked as I usually do, and went in. There was a poor young fellow lying in bed. He didn't look at all well. Suddenly the lights went out and we were in total darkness. The lad started screaming about how he was afraid of the dark. It was a pitiful sound. He kept asking for his mother. Well she wasn't there, of course, so I tried to console him. I sat near him and stroked his forehead. He hugged me tightly and—and . . .

Billy Go on.

Mum I'm sure he didn't know what he was doing.

Billy For a first timer, he seems to have been very successful.

Mum He didn't seem to regain his senses until the electrical power was restored. He then made a remarkable recovery. I didn't mention the incident to the authorities because I didn't want to embarass the poor chap. Anyway, it wasn't until much later that I discovered the outcome of it all.

Billy You mean me?

Mum Yes. Do you know, the strange thing about all this is that no-one else in the hotel reported a power cut. I can't help thinking I was had.

Billy In every sense of the word.

Mum You see, Aunty Ethel got it all wrong. She thought I was some shameless hussy slipping from hotel room to hotel room offering extra room service to the male guests.

Billy You can't deny, though, that you practically disowned me and did everything you could to get your hands on the money.

Mum I know. I suppose I just felt very bitter about the whole episode.

Billy (*suddenly noticing Annie*) What is that?

Mum That's Annie.

Billy Annie?

Mum Annie's the same age as you, Billy. She works in the launderette with me. Do you know, Billy, I'm sure you and Annie will have such a lot in common.

Billy We will?

Mum Once you get to know each other better.

Billy Hold on . . .

Mum There you are; two poor lost lambs thrown together. (*She sits him forcibly on the sofa*)

Billy Wait a minute . . .

Mum Clinging to each other—(*She puts Billy's arms around Annie*)—for refuge in this big bad world.

Billy (*releasing his hold on Annie*) No way.

Mum With me to help you and guide you and protect you . . .

Billy And spend my money for me! You cunning old . . .! I see your little plan. You get me married off to Little Orphan Annie here and move in as housekeeper. We accept you, of course, because we're so grateful for you introducing us. Before long you're running the house and you've got your grubby hands on the purse strings. (*Turning to Annie*) And you'll do quite well out of this, won't you? Suddenly whisked away from your dreary life in the launderette and thrown into the whirlwind life of your rich husband's world. Well, you've forgotten one tiny point. I'm supposed to be attracted to her. I'm supposed to *want* her, fancy her.

Mum Don't you feel for her? Don't you want to do something for her?

Billy Yes, sure. I could nominate her as a candidate for euthanasia.

Mum What's that?

Billy Putting people down when they're no use.

Annie Waah! (*She wails and cries*)

Mum Now look what you've done.

Billy That's it blame me. I didn't ask you to bring her here.

Annie cries loudly all the time

When I want to marry someone it'll be a girl of my own choice, not some myopic maiden presented to me as though I were a Bedouin tribesman waiting for his tenth wife. This is ridiculous. I mean, we're not in the Middle Ages are we?

Annie still wails

Oh shut up!

Annie abruptly stops crying

Mum Obviously we're not getting anywhere at the moment.

Billy And we're not likely to, either.

Mum I'm going to take Annie out . . .

Billy Good idea.

Mum And we'll be back later.

Billy Damn!

Mum Is there a solicitor dealing with the legacy?

Billy Yes. Some bloke by the name of Shoesmith. He had to go home but he'll be back this afternoon, about five o'clock I think. There are a few formalities to go through then the money will be handed over.

Mum We'll be back then. I'll leave you to think about this poor little child.

Billy Don't worry, I won't.

Mum You're a cruel boy, William Nelson.

Billy Wickedly cruel. I know.

Mum Your turn will come.

Billy It's been my turn for the last twenty-one years. I can't help thinking that it's someone else's turn now. (*He opens the door*) How about you two ladies. Come on now don't be shy, step this way for twenty years hard luck. Come on my dear.

Mum goes to the door

That's it, lady, bring your ugly dwarf with you.

Mum goes out

Annie follows, and stops in the doorway. She turns and looks at Billy

Oh by the way, there's a very busy road outside. You could easily get knocked down—with a bit of luck!

Annie Waah!

Wailing, Annie goes out

Billy shuts the door

Billy Whew! This place is turning into a madhouse. I need a drink.

He goes to pour out a drink. As he does so there is a knock at the door

Pat (*off*) Billy, let me in.

Billy opens the door

Pat enters

Billy Where have you been?

Pat Down in the basement. Sitting between two dustbins waiting for your mother to leave. Who lives in flat six?

Billy I've no idea. Why?

Pat His dustbin is absolutely full of nothing but empty tuna-fish tins.

Billy Perhaps he has a very big cat. Would you like a drink? (*He holds out a bottle*)

Pat No thank you. I don't want to tempt providence.

Billy How do you mean?

Pat Well, it was the demon drink that started all this muddle, wasn't it?

Billy (*thoughtfully*) Yes. Perhaps you're right. (*He returns the bottle*)

Pat What did Mummy want?

Billy The money, what else?

Pat What happened?

Billy Not a lot.

Pat Who was that girl?

Billy Oh, some creature she'd dragged in from somewhere. She wanted me to fall passionately in love with her, marry her and be eternally grateful for being introduced.

Pat And you would show your gratitude by sharing your legacy?

Billy Something like that.

There is a knock at the door

Now who's that?

Pat Why don't you open the door and see?

Billy Good thinking, Batman. (*He opens the door*)

Jane, a young woman, stands there. She is smartly dressed and attractive

Jane Mr Nelson?

Billy Yes.

Jane How do you do. My name's Jane Robinson, I'm Mr Shoesmith's secretary.

Billy Oh I see. Do come in.

Jane Thank you. (*She steps in*) Is Mr Shoesmith not here?

Billy I'm afraid not. He had to go home urgently. He wasn't feeling too good and he'd forgotten his glasses. He said he would be back this afternoon. I'm expecting him about five o'clock. Could I take a message for him?

Jane I'm sorry but what I have to see him about is confidential. I tried phoning him here from the office but I kept getting some jibbering idiot on the other end telling me to clear off because he was busy.

Billy and Pat exchange glances

Billy Why don't you phone him from here? (*He offers her the telephone*)

Jane It's worth a try, thank you. (*She takes the telephone, dials and waits*) No reply. He must have left home and started on his way back.

Jane Do you mind if I wait here until he returns? It is urgent.

Billy Not at all. Would you like a drink?

Jane (*sitting*) Thank you, yes. (*To Pat*) I see you work for the Post Office. Do you enjoy the work?

Pat Er—yes.

Jane How about the pay?

Pat (*mimicking Nigel*) Well it ain't easy without a bit of the ready. Me and the girl-friend are thinking of emigrating. It's supposed to be easier to get a bit of loot together on the other side of the world.

Billy looks up and smiles knowingly. Pat winks at him

Jane What a coincidence.

Pat Yeah, why's that?

Jane My boy-friend Nigel is a telegram boy and we've been thinking about the same thing.

Billy clatters the bottles in surprise

You might even know him. Nigel Branson—cheeky fellow, he is, about your size, actually.

Pat Nigel Branson. No, I can't say I've met him. Mind you, everyone looks alike in this uniform.

Jane Yes, I suppose you've got a point there! Oh my God!

Billy What's up?

Jane My car, it's on double yellow lines. Is there anywhere I can park it?
Billy There's a car park at the back of the flats. You can park safely there.
Jane Thanks. I won't be long.

Jane rumages in her bag, finds her keys and leaves. She does not close the door

Pat Now what?
Billy Well, you can't stay here dressed like that. She could start asking some very awkward questions.
Pat (*resigned*) I know. I'll hide in the bedroom. What are you going to do?
Billy I'll have to think of some way of getting rid of her. You'd better get out of sight before she comes back.

Pat reaches the bedroom door

Hang on! (*He hands her his mother's cases*) Take these with you, they're cluttering the place up out here.

Pat goes into the bedroom

Now act naturally Billy boy. Don't panic. The day's threequarters over and no-one suspects you. What do we do? Well, there'll be people here later on, they'll want coffee. (*He goes to the kitchen, takes a tray and takes some mugs off the shelf*) There'll be me, Mother, Orphan Annie, Shoesmith, his juicy secretary—(*Looking at the mugs*)—that should be enough. (*He comes downstage and kneels. He puts the tray down and starts tidying up the records, etc., with his back to the front door*)

A Policeman appears at the door. He knocks

Come in.

The Policeman knocks again

Come in, love.

The Policeman walks in and stands. Billy is still busy with coffee mugs and records. His back is still to the Policeman, he thinks it is Jane

Why don't you sit down, love? Take your shoes off and have a rest. I poured a drink out for you. It's by the chair.

The Policeman looks at it

You're quite safe, you know. I'm not going to molest you. Not today anyway, not here. That's not to say you're not attractive, you certainly are but things aren't easy for me. Of course, you realize that don't you? Up till today it's always been thoughts for me. Once I'm twenty-one things will be different. It's no fun you know. I walk down the street and I see someone like you with your smart clothes, your trim figure and your shapely thighs and I want to do things like put my arm around you, nibble your ear or pinch your bottom but I daren't. Someone would be bound to see us and that would be it, but tomorrow; tomorrow will be different, my word yes. I'll be twenty-one then and free to do what I want. Oh yes. (*He turns and sees the Policeman*) Oh hell!

Policeman Good afternoon, sir.

Billy Er—g—good afternoon. I—I'm sorry about—um ... I suppose you've come to look for some hanky-panky?

Policeman Hanky-panky, sir?

Billy Yes. Mr Shoesmith said that I would be examined and a Policeman would call and look for signs of hanky-panky.

Policeman And you didn't want to disappoint the boys in blue, did you, sir? Very obliging of you, sir, if I may say so. It's amazing the lengths to which the public will go to help a policeman sometimes. (*He takes out his notebook and pencil, licks his pencil and writes*) "—asked if I would like some hanky-panky!" (*He closes the book and puts it away*) Have you been examined yet, sir?

Billy No.

Policeman I thought not.

Billy You can tell?

Policeman Oh yes. We know the signs, sir. Actually, sir, I've called on a different matter altogether. I'm investigating the disappearance of a telegram boy named Nigel Branson. Apparently he was despatched this morning with a telegram to this address and has not yet reported back to head office. His employers are understandably distressed by his failure to return. They are responsible for his well being and he is now clocking up double pay on the overtime scale. Have you seen the said Nigel Branson, sir?

Billy Er—no.

Policeman You haven't seen a telegram boy at all, sir?

Billy No. Not at all.

Policeman Are you certain, sir?

Billy Positive.

Policeman In carrying out a preliminary reconnaissance of the premises I encountered two ladies. One was old, the other younger.

Billy Both of them ugly?

Policeman Exceedingly so, sir, but that is unimportant. One of them told me that a telegram boy was here.

Billy I can't think where they got that idea from.

Policeman Is there anyone here at all sir?

Billy Er—no—I'm completely alone.

Policeman Then you won't mind if I take a look around will you, sir? (*He begins walking slowly around with some deliberation*)

Billy Take a look around?

Policeman Yes sir. Just to satisfy myself that the young man is not on the premises.

Billy But honestly, officer, I can assure you there is no telegram boy here.

Policeman So you keep saying sir. (*He examines the kitchen area*) I can't understand how he never arrived here, especially as his motor-bike is outside.

Billy Motor-bike?

Policeman Outside.

Billy Outside?

Policeman Outside.

Billy Perhaps he's still on his way up.

Policeman I would have overtaken him on the way, surely?

Billy Then perhaps he's gone too far.

Policeman In which case he will be carefully tip-toeing along the roof-tops looking for you, sir?

Billy Eh?

Policeman You live on the top floor, don't you?

Billy Then where could he be?

Policeman I'll ask the questions if you don't mind, Mr Nelson.

Billy I'm sorry I can't help you, constable, but . . .

Pat sneezes, off

Policeman Excuse me, sir, but I distinctly heard someone in that room.

Billy In there? Never.

Policeman Would that be your bedroom?

Billy Yes.

Policeman You wouldn't have a telegram boy ensconced in there would you, sir?

Billy Er . . .

There is a loud noise off—something is knocked over

Policeman There is someone in there. You have hidden Nigel Branson in your bedroom.

Billy (*dashing to the bedroom door and guarding it*) I haven't, I swear.

Policeman (*walking to the bedroom door*) I must ask you to move aside sir and allow me to inspect the room on the other side of this door!

Billy There's no telegram boy there!

Policeman Of course there isn't, sir. (*He moves Billy aside, straightens himself and knocks on the door*) Nigel Branson, are you there?

There is no reply

It's no good, I know you're in there. You may as well show yourself young man.

Pat appears in the doorway, dressed in woman's clothes

Pat Did *you* knock on the door, officer, or was it you, William?

Policeman (*looking embarrassed*) I'm terribly sorry, madam, I—er—thought there was a telegram boy in there.

Pat A telegram boy? Whatever gave you that idea? Would you care to take a look?

Policeman Um—no, miss, it's quite all right. I'm sorry to have bothered you. I'll continue my investigations elsewhere. (*He goes to the front door, and stops*) If a telegram boy should put in an appearance, sir, just send him back to his headquarters, would you?

Billy Yes, officer, I will, don't you worry.

The Policeman leaves

Billy shuts the door

How did you manage that?

Pat Simple. I opened one of the cases your mother left. I heard what the policeman was saying, so, obviously, I had to get out of Nigel's clothes.

Billy Speaking of Nigel . . .

Pat Oh my God . . .!

She runs to the wardrobe and opens it. Nigel is still standing there

Nigel, step out.

Nigel does so

Sit.

Nigel sits, and looks in a very sorry state

Billy Look at him. He doesn't know who he is, where he is or what day it is.

Pat Just as well for us he doesn't.

Billy Well we can't leave him sitting there can we? I mean, Shoesmith's secretary is going to come back any minute and I know your treatment will make *him* believe that he's the Prime Minister, a bag of worms and everything in between, but there's no way we will convince her that he's anything other than Nigel Branson, her boy-friend.

Pat (*thoughtfully*) There might be a way.

Billy Never!

Pat Do you want to bet? You've given me an idea. Watch this. Nigel, stand.

Nigel stands

You are a woman.

Nigel holds his hands in front of him, adopts a female stance and purses his lips

You have long dark hair.

Nigel tosses imaginary hair and runs his fingers through it

You are not yet dressed.

Nigel looks shocked and attempts to cover himself

You must go to the bedroom and get dressed.

Nigel walks in an effeminate way into the bedroom

He will too. Don't forget we've got two cases full of clothes to choose from.

Pat goes to the bedroom

Billy You're crackers. Absolutely bonkers. We won't get away with this you know. No-one in their right mind would ever . . .

Pat (*coming into the room with the telegram outfit*) Shut up and get rid of this. It's Nigel's uniform.

Pat puts Shoesmith's spectacles back in his briefcase and places the case behind the sofa, then goes into the bedroom

Billy Just like that. "Get rid of this," she says. I ask you, where am I supposed to put it?

There is a knock at the door. Billy opens it

Jane stands outside

Billy holds the uniform behind his back

Yes?
Jane It's me, Jane.
Billy Oh.
Jane Well, can I come in?
Billy Um—must you?
Jane Well, you did agree I could wait until Mr Shoesmith returns. Is it not now convenient?
Billy (*backing away from her*) Er, yes, yes, come in, do. Sit down, over there.

As Jane walks to her seat, Billy keeps his distance, he circles the room, facing her all the time with the uniform held behind him

Jane Are you all right? Don't you trust me, or something? I won't harm you or make advances. I've got a boy-friend. He's a bit of a wild lad, but I've no intention of running after other blokes. Just relax.
Billy (*standing stiffly*) I am.
Jane What have you got behind your back?
Billy Nothing. Just my hands, look. (*He shows her one hand, then the other, then backs slowly towards the front door*) I've just got to pop out for a moment. (*Still backing to the door*) I shouldn't be many minutes. (*He stands with his back to the wall near the door and reaches out to open it*) Make yourself comfortable. (*He opens the door*)

The Policeman is standing there

Policeman I'm sorry to bother you again, sir.
Billy Ah, ah, ah! (*He turns and doubles up, clutching the uniform to his middle*)
Policeman (*stepping right inside*) I didn't intend to frighten you, sir.
Jane Are you all right? (*To the Policeman*) I thought he was behaving strangely.
Policeman You as well, eh, miss?
Jane Can I get you something?
Billy Um—yes, please.
Jane A drink?
Billy Yes.

Jane goes to the kitchen and returns with a glass of water

Jane Here you are.
Billy It's no good. (*Flustered*) It's—it's—the wrong colour.
Jane The wrong colour?
Billy Yes.

Jane looks at the glass, puzzled

Policeman (*taking her to one side*) I think you'd better humour him, miss.
Jane Humour him?

The Policeman nods

Why, you don't think he's—?
Policeman —as a fruit cake, if you ask me. Better get him some more water.

Jane does so as the Policeman speaks

We're just getting you a different glass of water, sir. We'll feel better then, won't we, sir?
Billy Will we? Are *you* ill?
Policeman If you say so, sir.
Billy What do you mean, if I say so?
Policeman If it makes you feel any better, then I'll be ill.
Billy What the hell are you jibbering on about? You'll be ill to make me better? What do you think I am, a voodoo witch doctor or something?
Jane Here's your drink.
Billy Um. Put it down by the door please.

Jane looks at Policeman, he nods his approval, so she carefully places the glass by the open front door

Thanks, why don't you both sit down?

Jane and the Policeman sit. Billy, still bent double begins inching his way towards the glass

Jane What shall we do?
Policeman Leave him, miss. At least he's not violent. These blokes have got the strength of nine men. If he goes wild he'll outnumber us by seven to two.

Billy reaches the door, and gives a cry of triumph

Billy Ha, ha!

Billy scuttles away

Jane Surely he's not completely mad.
Policeman Not my place to say, really, miss. Can't be too sure though, can we?
Jane I think you've made a mistake, officer. He was talking to me quite

normally when I was here earlier. He was quite chatty, him and his friend.

Policeman His friend, miss?

Jane Yes, a telegram boy.

Policeman (*standing and taking out his notebook*) A thin wiry man, a cheeky look on his face, engaging personality, always had a ready answer?

Jane Sounds like him.

Policeman (*putting his notebook away*) You're sure he was here, miss?

Jane I'm going mad if he wasn't.

Policeman In this place, that wouldn't be impossible.

Jane (*laughing*) No, seriously, there was a telegram boy here, I spoke to him, he told me of his intentions to emigrate to Australia.

Policeman That's the one I'm looking for. Thank you, miss, you've been a great help. I have reason to believe that a certain telegram boy has been abducted by Mr William Nelson. He might easily have murdered the boy, chopped him into pieces and at this very moment be forcing the pieces into a waste disposal unit.

Jane Why on earth would he do that?

Policeman To destroy the evidence.

Jane No—kill him in the first place?

Policeman Because he's mad. Simple as that.

Jane (*shivering*) Ooh, it gives me the creeps. To think, if the telegram boy had gone and left me here, it would be me being fed into the waste disposal unit.

Policeman Either that or your body stored in a deep freezer until he can find a convenient way to dispose of it. They do that you know, these psychopaths.

Jane Poor lad.

Policeman Yes. A fellow by the name of Branson.

Jane (*shocked*) Did—did you say Branson?

Policeman Yes, miss.

Jane Nigel Branson?

Policeman That would be him, miss.

Jane But Nigel Branson is my boy-friend.

Policeman And you were talking to him, here, but failed to recognize him?

Jane No, the person I spoke to was someone else, not Nigel at all.

Policeman But Nigel Branson was the boy asked to deliver the telegram.

They stand in silence

My God, you know what this means?

Jane What?

Policeman There were *two* telegram boys! He's done 'em both in! One down the waste disposal pipe and the other in a freezer somewhere. The perverted swine. He's got a fetish about telegram boys, he lures them to his flat and then commits his dastardly deeds.

Jane Oh my Nigel, my poor, poor Nigel.

Policeman Now that he's been found out he could well turn violent. We must be on our guard continually. Remember, we must do nothing to arouse his suspicions until the time is right. I will use my professional judgement, speedy assessment of each situation and deductive thought to choose that time.

Jane Pardon?

Policeman Leave it all to me.

Jane Oh I see.

There is a noise from the bedroom

What was that?

Policeman Excuse me Miss. (*He points to the door*) The fellow has a fancy lady in his room. It's about time we offered her some protection.

Jane A fancy woman. I thought he was supposed to be leading a life of purity.

Policeman Just a front, a cunning trick not to show his real self.

Billy enters

Billy Ah, that's better. I'm sorry I had to make such a strange exit. I suddenly had to leave. There was—er—something I—um—had to get rid of.

The Policeman and Jane look at each other

What did you want, anyway, officer?

Policeman Just calling by, sir, to tell you that my search for the missing telegram boy had been in vain. The lad must have gone home.

Billy Oh, I see. Well, that clears up that little problem.

Policeman And you haven't seen a telegram boy at all today, sir?

Billy (*angrily*) No, I keep telling you. What do you think I'm doing? Enticing hordes of telegram boys to my home in order to have my way with them?

Policeman I didn't say that, sir. Is your—um—"Friend" still in your room, sir?

Billy (*looking worried*) Friend?

Policeman Yes, sir. The young lady we met earlier.

Billy begins to look anxious

Jane It's quite all right, Mr Nelson. This will make no difference to the outcome of your legacy.

Billy Oh, I see. Well, yes, actually she is, but . . .

Policeman Thank you, sir. (*He knocks on the bedroom door*) Would you mind coming out, please.

There is a pause, then the door slowly opens and Pat comes from the bedroom, followed by Nigel dressed in a dress and wig. He carries a handbag and looks dazed

Everyone stares in amazement

Policeman (*removing his helmet and scratching his head*) Blimey, he's got two of 'em in there.

Billy I think I can explain, officer.

Policeman (*disbelievingly*) Well, it might be worth a try I suppose. Pass a few desultory moments so to speak. Liven the proceedings.

Billy Look, this is Pat . . .

Pat And this is my sister, Brenda.

Policeman Oh, I see, keep it in the family, eh?

Pat Brenda and I go everywhere together.

Policeman Is that so—um—Brenda?

Nigel (*in a deep, female voice*) Yes, everywhere.

Policeman I see, and I'll bet you have a lot of fun together.

Nigel I'm not that sort of girl. I'll have you know I'm an ex-member of the Brownies.

Pat She has a religious leaning, you see, officer. She sees it her personal duty to protect me.

Policeman I see, and when did you first feel this need to follow a "religious" path?

Nigel When I saw a relevation on the television screen.

Policeman You saw the Almighty on television?

Nigel No, I don't think it was God who actually spoke to me.

Policeman Then who was it?

Nigel Michael Parkinson.

Policeman Oh, he counts as God! Clearly you have had a religious experience. I commend your protective attitude, miss.

Shoesmith appears at the door. He is wearing his glasses and carrying a crash helmet and the telegram boy's uniform

Shoesmith What on earth is going on here?

Jane (*running to him, crying*) Oh, Mr Shoesmith . . .

Shoesmith Miss Robinson, what are you doing here? Really, this is a most unusual day. I got out of the taxi and as I was walking around to the car park this crash helmet landed on my head.

Policeman Thrown from a window in this block of flats I would suggest, sir.

Shoesmith I would think so. Who are you?

Policeman Police Constable Carter sir. Would those be the jacket and trousers of a telegram boy, sir?

Shoesmith I really couldn't tell you, officer. Telegram boys are not my line of country. I found them stuffed through the window of my car.

Pat (*to Billy*) You idiot!

Billy I didn't know it was his car!

Policeman Before we go any further I feel it is my duty to explain why I am here. In the course of my day's duties I was told that a certain telegram boy had failed to report to his superiors after being despatched to this address. I have been unable to locate the boy, a certain Nigel Branson, but it would seem that you have found his clothes, sir.

Shoesmith (*examining the clothes*) It looks that way.

Policeman May I ask exactly who you are, sir?

Shoesmith My name is Shoesmith. Rodney Shoesmith. I'm a solicitor. I'm here to discuss some business with Mr Nelson.

Policeman (*to Billy*) Very quick work on your part, getting a solicitor over here so soon.

Shoesmith I was here this morning.

Policeman Actually called in his solicitor before comitting the offence. Very astute.

Billy (*to Pat*) What's he talking about? I haven't comitted any offence.

Policeman I'll be the judge of that, if you don't mind.

Shoesmith Are we going to assume you are now searching for a naked telegram boy, officer?

Policeman No sir. I don't think so. I was about to explain, I was sent here to look for the missing lad. My suspicions have been aroused and I believe there is a little more to all this than meets the eye. (*Waving around the room*) Ladies and gentlemen. I want you to prepare yourselves for a shock, a very nasty shock.

Mum appears in the doorway with Annie. Annie is now without her beret and raincoat. She is dressed outlandishly in extreme fashion. She still wears her glasses

Mum Billy darling, we're back.

They come in

Now feast your eyes on this beauty. I'm sure that Annie would be the first to admit she didn't look her best this morning, but now, you've got to admit, she looks a different sight altogether.

Billy I'd agree with that.

Mum I decided that you young things don't appreciate each other unless you're dressed in up-to-the-minute fashion.

Billy Go on.

Mum So first of all we went to the *boutique* . . .

Billy And bought up the rejects.

Mum Then we visited the beauty parlour . . .

Billy Which was closed, I see.

Mum Then came back here.

Policeman You are the lady I met earlier in the day at the foot of the stairs?

Mum Why yes. Have you been here all that time?

Policeman (*taking out his notebook*) Who exactly are you, madam?

Mum Margarette Nelson.

Billy My mother.

Policeman You have my sympathies.

Mum } Thank you. { (*Speaking together*)
Billy }

Billy That's Annie.

Mum Soon to be *Mrs William Nelson*.

Billy Over my dead body.

Policeman An interesting choice of phrase. (*He notes it down*)

Billy What are you doing?

Policeman Making a few notes, sir.

Billy What for?

Policeman Well, I'll give you a clue sir. I'm *not* on the research team for "This Is Your Life".

Billy Look, she's trying to get me married off to that, that—simpleton. I'd rather be hanged for murder than spend my days with her.

Policeman (*writing in his book again*) Would you now, sir?

Shoesmith Look, I apologize for appearing dim.—

Policeman That's quite all right, sir.

Shoesmith —but what is going on?

Policeman Well, sir, I was about to explain. I was called to search for the missing Nigel Branson . . .

Annie Oh, he's such a nice man.

Policeman Nigel Branson?

Annie No! Eamonn Andrews.

The others look at one another, perplexed

Shoesmith How the heck did *he* get into the conversation? No-one's talking about Eamonn Andrews.

Mum No-one even mentioned him, dear.

Annie Yes, they did.

Policeman Who did?

Annie (*to the policeman*) You did.

Policeman Me?

Annie Yes.

Policeman I didn't.

Annie Yes, you did.

Policeman Oh blood and sand! When?

Annie You were talking about "This Is Your Life".

Shoesmith I'm cracking up! I know I am. I had my suspicions this morning.

Billy And she wants me to marry that!

Policeman Strictly off the record, sir, I can understand your consternation. However we are not here to discuss your potential marital problems.

Shoesmith I agree. We are here on a much more serious business. Officer I shall have to ask you to stay for a little longer to clear up some business.

Policeman Don't worry sir, I intend to.

Shoesmith Good. Now where shall we start?

Policeman Where I left off sir. I have reason to believe that one or more telegram boys have been lured to this address, their subsequent re-appearance has not been witnessed, so I therefore believe that these poor innocent people have quite possibly been murdered and their bodies disposed of in a most vile way.

There is a momentary silence

Billy But who could have done such a thing?

Policeman } You! { (*Speaking together*)
Jane

The Lights fade to a Black-out, and—

the CURTAIN *falls*

ACT III

The same. Some time later

Pat and Billy are on the sofa, Nigel is sitting on the pouffe, Annie and Mum are standing behind the sofa, with Shoesmith and Jane beside them. The Policeman is facing them, downstage

Policeman Now, sir. My work may take some time so I am willing to allow you to complete your business first though, why this villain should remain free a moment longer I do not understand.

Billy I keep telling you. I am innocent.

Policeman That's what Christie said, sir.

Billy Oh no. What do you think I've done, bricked 'em up in the wall?

Policeman (*taking out notebook*) A possibility I hadn't entertained. (*He writes*) Check dimensions of room.

Mum You evil little swine.

Billy God. Accused, tried and pronounced guilty in one easy move. Why don't you put me on a horse, take me to the outskirts of town and lynch me?

Shoesmith Don't be silly. We have to clear up this other business first. Let me explain the situation officer. (*He looks around*) Is my briefcase still here?

Mum (*holding up the briefcase from behind the sofa*) Is this it?

Shoesmith Ah, thank you. (*He takes the briefcase, opens it and finds his glasses*) Ah—ah . . . (*He cries out*)

Pat What's wrong?

Shoesmith My glasses are in here.

Policeman Hardly an observation for such hysteria.

Shoesmith But—but—I—I— . . . Oh. (*He groans*) I think I'll take a holiday after this.

Policeman I think that's a good idea, sir.

Shoesmith (*putting his glasses in his pocket*) Where was I?

Billy Going on holiday.

Policeman Not just yet, I'm afraid. Though I wouldn't be surprised if you'd contemplated skipping the country.

Shoesmith As a matter of fact, officer, he has recently obtained a passport.

Billy Oh for goodness sake! I don't believe it.

Policeman I could believe just about anything at the moment m'lad. Now, you were going to explain.

Shoesmith Ah yes. This young man—(*indicating Billy*)—has been left a substantial sum of money which he is due to inherit on his twenty-first birthday . . .

Jane That's why I'm here.

Shoesmith That's why we're all here, dear. Let me finish. But he may only inherit it if he has remained pure until that time.

Policeman "Pure", sir?

Pat What we, on the other side of the fence, refer to as *"virgo intacta"*.

Policeman I understand, miss, thank you. Do continue.

Shoesmith I have established, beyond any doubt, that he is indeed Mr William Nelson.

Policeman Good! That'll save me a job later on.

Billy rises in anger. Pat pulls him down

Shoesmith He has to be examined to establish that he is—uh—hum—(*he coughs*)—what the young lady said.

Policeman You're not asking me to do that, sir?

Shoesmith No. You are to investigate the premises to ascertain whether there is any evidence pointing towards any goings on which a medical examination may have overlooked.

Policeman There will be no need to do that, sir.

Shoesmith What do you mean?

Policeman I mean, sir, that what I have seen here today points towards a distinct *lack* of purity.

Shoesmith This is most distressing. However, please continue.

Policeman Firstly I have no doubt that this "person" has a distastful liking for people of his own sex.

Shoesmith This ties in with what I saw this morning.

Policeman Really sir?

Shoesmith Yes there was a lithesome young fellow cavorting around in his underpants. I was willing to give Mr Nelson the benefit of the doubt at the time but you have obviously seen more.

Policeman Indeed I have, sir. When I first entered the premises Mr Nelson made his intentions abundantly clear.

Billy What?

Policeman He displayed a liking for men in uniform . . .

Shoesmith Which explains his fascination for telegram boys.

Policeman Very astute of you, sir.

Shoesmith Thank you. I normally deal in conveyancing you know?

Policeman I'd hardly have guessed. Before I could make it clear I was not his for the asking he said—(*he refers to his book*)—he would "like to nibble my ear".

Shoesmith What?

Policeman And pinch my bottom.

Mum Did you say that?

Billy Yes, but . . .

Mum You dirty little devil.

Billy Oh Lord . . .

Policeman In spite of my refusals and a jocular attempt to make light of the proceedings and thus avoid an embarrassing incident, he persisted.

Billy I did?

Policeman He offered me some—(*he looks at his book*)—"hanky-panky"!

Shoesmith Is there more, officer?

Policeman I'm afraid there is sir. Mr Nelson has also been entertaining young *ladies* in his bedroom.

Shoesmith (*incredulously*) Boys *and* girls. Now listen to me, young fellow. It's high time you made up your mind as to which truck you're going to jump on. You can't dither around at your age chasing men one minute and women the next. You don't know where you'll end up or what'll happen to you. You could go blind—anything. Now, officer, you were telling me about these women.

Policeman Quite sir. When I first called about the missing boy, Nigel Branson.

Jane Wah!

Jane wails, making Shoesmith start

Shoesmith Why did you do that?

Policeman Branson is her boy-friend, sir.

Mum Oh, my poor dear! (*Going to comfort her*) I don't know what to say. To think that my own son should cause this . . . If I could disown him, I would.

Billy Again?

Shoesmith When you called about Branson?

Policeman And he attempted to lure me to his room, he also had a young lady in there.

Mum You're no son of mine.

Policeman When I called later, her sister was in there with her.

Shoesmith (*to Billy*) Where do you get the strength from? That's what I want to know?

Pat Beans, mashed potato and creamed rice.

Billy (*laughing*) Yeh, that's right.

Pat With a good dose of Andrews for that extra oomph!

Billy (*stopping laughing*) Oh hell, why am *I* laughing?

Shoesmith (*to Pat*) I don't think we've actually met.

Pat I'm Pat.

Policeman And this is her sister Brenda. The two girls in question, sir.

Shoesmith (*examining Nigel*) She looks as though she's coming out of a hangover rather than an orgy.

Billy There never was an orgy!

Shoesmith Which might explain the look of disappointment on her face. Is there any more, officer?

Policeman No sir, that is it.

Shoesmith (*disappointedly*) Oh.

Mum Isn't that plenty? There's enough material there for a remake of Sodom and Gemorrah. Surely there's no doubt he has broken the requirements of the legacy?

Billy I haven't. There's nothing wrong with me.

Shoesmith What would you say about a person who keeps semi-naked men in his room, solicits policemen and associates with women who shave twice a day?

Billy I'd say there was something wrong with him.

Shoesmith There you are.

Mum He's admitted it! It's his twenty-first birthday. He hasn't done as the will says so the money comes to me. That's right, isn't it?

Shoesmith Yes, I suppose it does.

Jane No, it doesn't.

Mum What! Why not?

Jane All this could have been avoided if I had been allowed to speak earlier. Mr Shoesmith, would you please read the requirements of the will?

Shoesmith Is that necessary?

Jane Yes. Read it please. (*She hands him the will from his briefcase*)

Shoesmith All of it?

Jane Just the important bit.

Shoesmith (*reading*) "—and to my little Willy—"

Billy That's me.

Shoesmith "—I bequeath the remainder of my estate which shall not come into his legal possession until his twenty-first birthday. It shall pass to his mother, Margarette, on that day if he has not until that time, remained bodily pure and free of all carnal knowledge."

Billy So?

Jane Well, it's very clear.

Policeman It is?

Jane Yes. Billy, when is your birthday?

Billy Today. I'm twenty-one today.

Jane Yes, I know you're twenty-one today but is this your twenty-first birthday?

Shoesmith Really, Miss Robinson, I don't know what you're driving at.

Jane When were you born?

Billy Nineteen fifty-six.

Jane And the date?

Billy February the twenty-ninth.

Jane Well, there you are.

Mum He was a leap year baby. We all know that, it's on his birth certificate What does that prove?

Jane That no-one can have the money.

Mum Rubbish. It's all written down. "It shall not come into his possession until he's twenty-one. It shall pass to his mother, Margarette . . ."

Jane Wrong! (*She snatches the will from Shoesmith and reads*) It shall not come into his possession until his twenty-first *birthday*. His birthday is on February the twenty-ninth. Today is *not* February the twenty-ninth.

Billy Then how many birthdays have I really had?

Jane Five.

Billy (*laughing*) And how long must I remain pure to claim the money?

Jane Another sixty-four years.

Billy My God I'll be eighty-five. It'll be too late!

Mum What are you complaining about? I'll be a hundred and two!

Billy (*laughing*) Oh boy that's great. I've been preserving myself for the last twenty-one years, she's been bending over backwards to lay her hands on the loot, and no-one can get a penny of it.

Pat Well, that's the end of this little problem, isn't it.

Policeman Not quite, I'm afraid, miss. There is still the matter of the two telegram boys.

Billy There was only one telegram boy.

Policeman Well, we'll start with him, then, shall we, sir? What did you do with the body? You couldn't have flushed it down the lavatory.

Billy Look, nobody died.

Shoesmith You've already admitted there was a telegram boy. Why don't you own up to it lad? You've nothing to gain now. Come on, make a clean breast of it.

Jane Oh my poor, poor Nigel. (*Weeping*) I know you weren't the best of lads but, you were all that I had. I loved you Nigel, I really did. We were going to have such good times together but now that monster has put an end to it all.

Jane sinks to her knees, while the others gather around, leaving Nigel on the pouffe behind their backs

The only person I ever loved. (*Looking upwards*) I know you're still here Nigel, still with me. You'll always be with me and I'll always be waiting. One day, Nigel darling, we'll be together again.

Nigel is now sober. He is looking around perplexed

And then we'll be happy for ever and ever. Oh Nigel, I can't wait for that happy day. The guardian angel will open those pearly gates—

Everyone looks overcome, handkerchiefs appear

—I will step through to the sound of harps playing and the sweet singing of cherubim and seraphim. A cloud will float down and you will be riding on it. You will take me by the hand, stare into my eyes and say those beautiful words . . .

Nigel Where the bleedin' 'ell am I?

Everyone looks amazed. There is a pause

Jane Oh Nigel, is that really you?

Nigel 'Course it's me. Who do you think it is?

Everyone turns to Nigel

Shoesmith She's speaking with a man's voice.

Jane It's Nigel's voice!

Mum She's a medium. That's what she is. The man is contacting you through her. Quickly, we must all hold hands.

They do so. Billy and Pat try to refuse but they are drawn in

Let me handle this. (*She speaks in a slow clear voice as if talking to a child*) Nigel Branson, do you have a message for anyone here?

Nigel Yeh—for Mr William Nelson. (*He looks puzzled*)

Mum (*to Billy*) It's for you. What is the message, Nigel?

Nigel I don't know.

Mum Why don't you know, Nigel?

Nigel We're not allowed to open the envelope.

Everyone looks puzzled

Billy Oh Christ! He's talking about the blasted telegram he brought this morning. (*He steps forward*) Look this isn't a girl called Brenda. (*He rips the wig off Nigel*) This *is* Nigel Branson.

Jane Oh Nigel! (*She rushes to him, kisses him and kneels down beside him*)

Billy There! Are you satisfied now that I didn't kill Nigel Branson?

Policeman (*reluctantly*) I suppose you're right, sir.

Billy Well, don't sound so cheerful, what's the matter?

Policeman I was banking on a little promotion from this. (*He sits wearily, then rises*) Wait a minute, though. What did you do with the other telegram boy?

Billy There wasn't another telegram boy.

Jane Yes there was, I saw him.

Mum So did I.

Pat That was me.

Shoesmith You don't look like a boy to me.

Pat Well, how about this. (*She puts on the crash helmet and speaks in a deep voice*) We always open the telegrams now, read 'em, an' if it's bad news, rip 'em up!

Mum That's him all right, isn't it, Annie?

Annie nods

Shoesmith But why were you dressed as a boy?

Jane (*still near Nigel*) And why was he dressed as a woman?

Billy It's a long, long story.

Pat Billy had a party here last night and I had my clothes stolen.

Billy (*pointing to Nigel*) By him.

Jane (*to Nigel*) You said you were working late last night. Out on a job, you said.

Shoesmith It doesn't sound as if he was far wrong to me.

Billy I had too much to drink and flaked out.

Pat And I had to stay the night on the sofa.

Policeman Because your clothes had been stolen?

Pat Right.

Billy When I woke up this morning, Pat was still here.

Pat Unclothed.

Billy (*to Jane*) You phoned to say Mr Shoesmith was on his way round.

Nigel And that's when I arrived with a telegram.

Mum To say that I would be arriving today.

Nigel It was all my fault originally so I agreed to let her borrow my clothes.

Shoesmith So I wouldn't think a woman had stayed the night here!

Billy Correct.

Shoesmith What a brilliant idea. If this was all written down it would make a marvellous play.

Pat No! No-one would believe it.

Annie begins to cry

Mum My love what's wrong?

They help her to sit on the sofa, and all stand around

Annie What's going to happen to me?

Shoesmith What do you mean, dear?

Annie There's no-one to look after me.

Billy (*raising his arms*) Ahh!

Pat Shut up you fool! Why isn't there anyone to look after you?

Annie Well, my mother's dead.

Policeman (*interested*) Really?

Billy Don't look at me. It's nothing to do with me.

Annie She died when I was seven.

Policeman Your father's dead as well?

Annie I don't know.

Shoesmith Why not?

Annie I was conceived in an hotel.

Billy You as well?

Annie Yes. I thought it a strange coincidence when your mother explained her brief encounter with your father. You see, the same sort of thing happened to my mother. She was working in an hotel in Norwich when, one night, as she was turning down the sheets, there was a power cut. There was a man in the same room as her at the time. He was afraid of the dark, so she tried to comfort him and he had his way with her.

Shoesmith This is amazing.

Policeman You're right, sir. Did she ever see the rascal again Miss?

Annie No, but on her death bed she gave me this key which I have worn around my neck ever since. (*She produces a key on a chain*) Apparently my father gave it to her and said it was the key to his heart.

Billy (*fumbling inside his shirt*) Is there an inscription on it?

Annie Yes.

Billy (*producing a similar key on a chain*) Mother, I've always worn this key. Where did it come from?

Mum (*in a quiet voice*) Your father gave it to me.

Billy What does the inscription say?

Annie (*looking at it closely and reading with some difficulty*) Take this key. It will open my heart . . .

Shoesmith I'll always think of you. Even when we're apart.

They look at Shoesmith

Policeman Are you familiar with these keys, sir?

Shoesmith I must admit I am. I bought a set of them from a street salesman when I was working in Cleethorpes. Whenever I was working away from home I would take the keys with me. I was younger then, you understand. I used to use the power cut routine in every hotel I stayed in. It never failed. I used to present a key to the young lady involved as a token of my appreciation. Those are undoubtedly two of them.

Mum Then you are the young man I fell for when working at the *Green Dragon*?

Shoesmith In Shrewsbury. Yes, I'm afraid I am.

Annie And I assume you also stayed at a hotel in Norwich?

Shoesmith I did. Yes. A very high class establishment called the *Royal*.

Billy Then you are my father?

Policeman He obviously is, sir.

Annie And mine too.

Shoesmith Yes.

Nigel fumbles about inside his dress

Billy (*to Annie*) Then you're my sister.

Annie Half-sister.

Billy Well, at least I won't have to *marry* you.

Nigel (*holding a key*) Take this key, it'll open my heart. I'll always think of you. Even when we're apart.

Policeman I beg your pardon, sir?

Nigel I've got one of those keys as well.

Shoesmith Oh no. This is going too far.

Policeman A bit late for such an observation I would think, sir.

Nigel I was born in Scunthorpe. I never knew my father either.

Billy Father, behold thy son. Child, behold thy . . .

Shoesmith Scunthorpe? Yes, I remember. I was there in nineteen fifty-seven. January.

Billy (*counting on his fingers*) Were you born in October?

Nigel Yes.

Billy No doubt about it. Child, behold thy father.

Policeman Are we to understand then, sir, that you are the father of these three people?

Shoesmith I don't honestly think I could deny it.

Jane Then you are to be my father-in-law, Mr Shoesmith.

Shoesmith I am? I mean am I? I mean—look out for the unexpected surprises, it said.

Mum What did?

Billy His horoscope.

Shoesmith I wasn't expecting this.

Policeman No, sir. I don't imagine you were.

Billy Well, here's another surprise for you. Dad; I'm going to get married.

Pat But Billy, you can't. She's your half-sister.

Billy Not to her, stupid.

Pat Then to whom?

Billy Throughout these proceedings there has been one person who has helped me. Through thick and thin she has unselfishly worked for what she believes is right—even at her own risk and peril. She is the kind of person I would be proud to call Mrs William Nelson. (*Turning to Pat*) Pat will you marry me?

Pat After a speech like that, I could hardly refuse, could I? Yes. I will.

Mum begins crying

Billy What are you so upset about?

Mum Nothing. I always cry at weddings.

Pat We're not actually at the altar yet.

Billy She's getting some practice in.

Nigel Well, brother.

Pat (*thumping Billy*) He's talking to you, stupid.

Billy Oh! Yes?

Nigel How do you feel about making it a double wedding?

Billy (*looking at Pat who nods in agreement*) Fine.

Nigel If that's okay with you, Dad?

Shoesmith Suddenly everyone's calling me Dad. I feel like a stud horse which has just returned home.

Policeman An interesting comparison, sir.

Nigel (*standing*) Well, this is indeed a happy day. I've found my father, a brother and sister, and I'm getting married.

Billy And the same goes for me, too.

Annie I've found my father and two strong brothers to care for me. I won't be alone any longer.

Mum (*to Shoesmith*) Well Casanova, are you going to hand out keys again, or have you come home to roost this time?

Shoesmith Oh no! My philandering days are long past. I'm a respectable man with an important position to think about.

Mum Then why don't we make it a triple wedding?

Shoesmith That would take some consideration, but at the moment, I see no reason why not.

Nigel Great. Then why don't we all go down to the pub on the corner—

Billy The *Pear Tree.*

Nigel —and celebrate?

Pat Good idea. Down to the *Pear Tree* it is.

Shoesmith I'll just collect my belongings and be with you in a moment.

All except Shoesmith and the Policeman begin to file out. Shoesmith stops Nigel and gives him his uniform

You'd better slip back into your proper clothes. No son of mine is going around dressed like a tart.

They leave

Shoesmith calls after them

And the first round is on me!

Billy (*off*) Thanks, Dad!

The Policeman and Shoesmith are left. Shoesmith collects his case, hat, etc.

Policeman What will happen to the money now, sir?

Shoesmith I'm not quite sure. I suppose there will have to be a meeting of all beneficiaries and some agreement made. Still, that can wait until Monday. Right now I've got a very thirsty family waiting in the lounge of the *Pear Tree*.

Policeman nervously shifts from one foot to the other

You look a little flustered, man. Was there something else?

Policeman Well, actually there was.

Shoesmith Well, come on then, out with it.

The Policeman loosens his tie and shirt

Policeman Well I'm not sure how to put this sir, but, were you in Salisbury in nineteen fifty-five?

Shoesmith Yes as a matter of fact I was. I stayed at the *Marlborough Hotel*. Why do you ask?

Policeman Well, I've got this key, sir.

Shoesmith And you never knew your father?

Policeman No, sir.

Shoesmith Well, I think you've just met him.

Policeman Yes, sir. I think I have.

Shoesmith sighs and walks towards the door, he turns to the Policeman

Shoesmith Well, you know where we all are. Are you going to join us— son?

Policeman I'll be right with you—Dad.

The Lights fade to a Black-out, and—

the CURTAIN *falls*

FURNITURE AND PROPERTY LIST

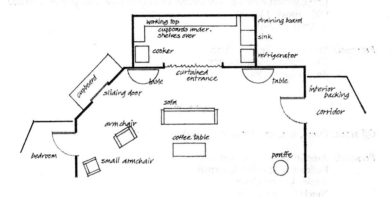

ACT I

On stage: SITTING-ROOM

Sofa. *On it:* cushions, blankets

Armchair

Small armchair

Pouffe

2 occasional tables. *On them:* record-player, records, empty and half-empty bottles, used glasses, full ashtrays, general remnants from a party

Coffee table. *On it:* bottles, glasses, ashtrays as above.

Carpet

On floor and generally around room: bottles, glasses, records, general party remnants

On front door: knocker

On floor by occasional table: telephone

KITCHEN ALCOVE

Practical sink. *On draining-board:* pre-set milk-bottle full of water, pre-set bowl full of water

Cooker

Refrigerator

Cupboards and shelves. *In and on them:* mugs, glasses, general dressing, various tins including instant mash, baked beans, creamed rice, Andrews Liver Salts

On floor: box containing catering size tins of baked beans, instant
   mash, creamed rice
Curtain across opening

Off stage: Telegram, notebook, crash helmet (**Nigel**)
   Brief case. *In it:* newspaper clipping, will, various documents and
      forms (**Shoestring**)
   Large brown envelope containing birth certificate and passport (**Billy**)
   Old suitcase (**Annie**)
   Suitcase (**Mum**)

Personal: **Billy:** sheet, key on chain
   Shoesmith: spectacles, pen
   Annie: spectacles

ACT II

Off stage: Dress, wig, handbag, set in bedroom (**Nigel**)

Personal: **Jane:** handbag with car keys
   Policeman: notebook, pencil
   Annie: key on chain
   Nigel: key on chain

LIGHTING PLOT

Property fittings required: wall brackets, kitchen strip (dressing only)
Interior. A sitting-room and kitchen. The same scene throughout

ACT I   Morning
To open: General effect of morning light
Cue 1   **Mum: "Billy!"**   (Page 21)
         Black-out

ACT II Morning
To open: As ACT I
Cue 2   **Policeman/Jane: "You!"**   (Page 38)
         Black-out

ACT III Morning
To open: As ACT I
Cue 3   **Policeman: "I'll be right with you—Dad"**   (Page 48)
         Black-out

EFFECTS PLOT

ACT I

ACT II

MADE AND PRINTED IN GREAT BRITAIN BY
LATIMER TREND & COMPANY LTD PLYMOUTH

MADE IN ENGLAND